MW01047702

TO

MoM with LOVE

FROM

SUSAN

DATE

8/28/93

LIFE'S SIMPLE PLEASURES

LIFE'S SIMPLE PLEASURES

Bruce Nash and Allan Zullo
and
Robyn Nash

THE SUMMIT GROUP ~ FORT WORTH, TEXAS

THE SUMMIT GROUP
1227 West Magnolia, Suite 500, Fort Worth, Texas 76104

Cataloging in Publication Data
(Prepared by Quality Books Inc.)

Nash, Bruce.
  Life's simple pleasures / Bruce Nash & Allan Zullo with Robyn Nash.

p. cm.

ISBN 1-56530-029-7

1. Self-help techniques. I. Zullo, Allan. II. Nash, Robyn. III. Title.

BF632.N37 1993   158.1
                          QB193-682

Jacket Design by Greg Ice

Manufactured in the United States of America
First Printing 1993

10   9   8   7   6   5   4   3   2   1

Stop to Smell the Roses

In the everyday hustle and bustle, we seldom take the time to appreciate the simple things in life.

Like playing fetch with a friendly dog. Catching rainwater in your mouth. Making a wish on the first star you see at night. Licking the bowl when making chocolate pudding.

By reflecting on those things which bring us joy, yet cost little or no money, we've compiled a list of over 500 simple pleasures in life. Naturally, everyone has his or her own idea of what constitutes a simple pleasure. What we hope to accomplish with our list is to give you a gentle reminder of all the wonderful experiences within your grasp that all too often are overlooked because of today's frantic pace.

So try taking a few minutes out of your busy schedule to experience these pleasurable moments. They're guaranteed to make each day of your life seem a little brighter.

Life's too short. Don't forget to stop and smell the roses!

• 1 •

Walking barefoot at dawn in a
dew-covered meadow.

• 2 •

Flying a kite on a windy day.

• 3 •

Designing a homemade greeting card—
the kind you used to make in elementary
school—for a loved one.

• 4 •

Marching in a parade.

• 5 •

Taking a small child to the circus.

• 6 •

A pillow fight.

• 7 •

Eating a banana split for your entire dinner.

• 8 •

Renting the black-and-white version
of *It's A Wonderful Life* and watching it with
your family on Christmas Eve.

• 9 •

Serving breakfast in bed to your mother.

• 10 •

Hearing the echo of your voice from atop a
mountain.

• 11 •

Seeing how many times you can make a
rock skip across a smooth lake.

• 12 •

Letting a friendly dog lick your face.

• 13 •

Playing hooky from work and going to a
movie you've been dying to see.

• 14 •

A big hug from a close friend.

• 15 •

Knowing that you are in someone's prayers
every night.

• 16 •

Going on a hayride.

• 17 •

Eating whatever you want while on vacation
without worrying about gaining weight.

• 18 •

Catching rainwater in your mouth.

• 19 •
Skipping.

• 20 •
Do-si-doing your partner at an old-fashioned square dance.

• 21 •
Lying under the night sky and spotting a
shooting star.

• 22 •
Wearing shiny shoes.

• 23 •

Putting a dollar of appreciation into a street musician's hat.

• 24 •

Fishing with an old cane pole and a can of worms.

• 25 •

Building a sand castle on the beach and then digging a moat around it so the incoming tide won't wash it away.

· 26 ·
Treating yourself to a long, leisurely
bubble bath.

· 27 ·
Eating homemade chocolate-chip cookies
hot from the oven with a big glass of milk.

· 28 ·
Skinny-dipping in a secluded lake.

· 29 ·
Buying a drink from a child's lemonade
stand.

• 30 •
Tossing a penny into a fountain and
making a wish.

• 31 •
A breakfast picnic in the park.

• 32 •
Telling spooky ghost stories around a
campfire.

• 33 •
Picking out a quiet, romantic spot
and watching the sun set with someone you
love.

• 34 •

Dressing up for Halloween in a scary
costume and going trick-or-treating with the
neighborhood kids.

• 35 •

Singing "The Star-Spangled Banner" out
loud at a sporting event.

• 36 •

Visiting the grave of a loved one if you
haven't been there lately.

◆ 37 ◆

Building a snowman.

◆ 38 ◆

A hunch that turns out to be right.

◆ 39 ◆

Eating cotton candy at the fair.

◆ 40 ◆

Making homemade popsicles with Kool-Aid
on a hot summer day.

• 41 •

Wishing upon the first star you see at night.

• 42 •

Winning at bingo.

• 43 •

Writing a love poem and reciting it to the special someone in your life.

• 44 •

Asking your lover out on a date, just like you did when you first met.

• 45 •
Reading a book to a blind person.

• 46 •
Paddling a canoe down a lazy river.

• 47 •
Drinking hot chocolate with
marshmallows on a cold winter night.

• 48 •
Buying yourself a balloon
and walking around the park with it.

• 49 •
Throwing a surprise birthday party for a
friend.

• 50 •
Showing your baby pictures to your kids.

• 51 •
Making angels in the snow.

• 52 •
Watching a Little League game
even if you don't know any of the kids
who are playing.

+ 53 +

Joining in an Easter egg hunt.

+ 54 +

Eating Chinese food with chopsticks.

+ 55 +

Having sweet nothings whispered in your
ear.

+ 56 +

Peeking at newborn babies in a
hospital's maternity ward.

• 57 •

Grabbing the brass ring on a merry-go-round.

• 58 •

Attending a free evening concert in the park.

• 59 •

Dressing up as Santa Claus for a yuletide party.

• 60 •

A candlelight dinner with your lover even though it's not a special occasion.

• 61 •

A kitten purring.

• 62 •

Cooking a favorite dish that your mother
used to make when you were young.

• 63 •

Getting a pedicure.

• 64 •

Fast forwarding through the
commercials when you play back videotapes
of your favorite TV programs.

♦ 65 ♦
Getting a call from an old friend you haven't
spoken with since high school.

♦ 66 ♦
Picking fresh flowers.

♦ 67 ♦
A babbling brook.

♦ 68 ♦
Sitting in front of a roaring fire
on a freezing night.

• 69 •
"Walking the dog" with a yo-yo.

• 70 •
Drinking a chocolate malt
at an old-fashioned soda shop.

• 71 •
Watching the space shuttle take off
and land safely.

• 72 •
Dancing the night away.

LIFE'S SIMPLE PLEASURES

• 73 •
Early-bird dinner specials.

• 74 •
Hopping to the finish line first in a sack
race.

• 75 •
Spotting a deer in the woods.

• 76 •
Listening to a bowl of Rice Krispies
"snap, crackle and pop."

• 77 •
Eating a red M & M.

• 78 •
Sinking a birdie putt on the first hole.

• 79 •
Receiving an income tax refund.

• 80 •
Using all of your Scrabble letters
to form a bonus word.

◆ 81 ◆
A sharp pencil.

◆ 82 ◆
Going on a scavenger hunt.

◆ 83 ◆
Raiding the refrigerator for a midnight
snack.

◆ 84 ◆
Completing the entire *New York Times*
crossword puzzle—in pen.

◆ 85 ◆
Roasting chestnuts over an open fire.

◆ 86 ◆
The smell of freshly mowed grass.

◆ 87 ◆
Walking barefoot on a soft, plush carpet.

◆ 88 ◆
Voting for the winning candidate
in a Presidential election.

• 89 •
Doing the wave at a football game.

• 90 •
A trouble-free Friday the 13th.

• 91 •
Eating an ice cream cone covered
with chocolate sprinkles.

• 92 •
Finding someone at home
who can help you carry in the groceries.

• 93 •
Kicking a can down the street.

• 94 •
Licking a candy cane.

• 95 •
Watching fish swim in an aquarium.

• 96 •
Finding out whether that certain someone
"loves you" or "loves you not" by picking the
petals one by one off a flower.

• 97 •
Drinking sun tea.

• 98 •
Sitting on the edge of a dock and splashing
your feet around in the water.

• 99 •
Visiting the old neighborhood
where you grew up.

• 100 •
Sleeping in the nude.

♦ 101 ♦
Snuggling under a down comforter.

♦ 102 ♦
The aroma from peeling an orange.

♦ 103 ♦
Winning a friendly wager.

♦ 104 ♦
Renting the only remaining copy
of a hard-to-find video.

• 105 •
Being told "I love you."

• 106 •
Being dealt a royal flush in a poker game.

• 107 •
Figuring out how to program your VCR.

• 108 •
Blowing "smoke" with your breath
on a chilly day.

• 109 •
Zooming down a hill on a toboggan.

• 110 •
Playing catch with your dad.

• 111 •
Letting out a big yawn.

• 112 •
Finding money in the pocket of your pants
after they've been washed.

• 113 •
Winning a prize at the fair.

• 114 •
No bills in the mail.

• 115 •
Receiving a "happy-to-see-you" greeting
from your dog after a hard day at work.

• 116 •
Winning a game of tic-tac-toe.

• 117 •
A flattering photo on your driver's license.

• 118 •
Correctly answering the "Final Jeopardy"
question.

• 119 •
Being surprisingly entertained by a movie
that you were dragged to see.

• 120 •
Drinking cold lemonade on a sweltering day.

• 121 •
Button candy.

• 122 •
The cool breeze of a fan blowing on your
face on a hot summer day.

• 123 •
A picnic with no flies or ants.

• 124 •
Being in love.

• 125 •

Finally getting rid of your hiccups.

• 126 •

Finding a lost sock.

• 127 •

The gentle sounds of wind chimes.

• 128 •

A fellow Monopoly player landing on your
Boardwalk property with a hotel on it.

• 129 •
Diving for pennies at the bottom of a pool.

• 130 •
Turning on the radio and hearing that your
favorite song is about to be played.

• 131 •
Forgetting your umbrella on a day it was
supposed to rain, but didn't.

• 132 •
Catching a fish and then eating it for dinner.

• 133 •
Singing "Jingle Bells" while riding
in a one-horse open sleigh.

• 134 •
The sand squishing through your toes
as you walk along the beach.

• 135 •
Grandchildren.

• 136 •
Pitching a ringer in horseshoes.

◆ 137 ◆
Looking in the sports section of the
morning newspaper and finding out that
your favorite team won last night's game.

◆ 138 ◆
Fixing a leak all by yourself and avoiding an
expensive repair job.

◆ 139 ◆
Browsing around in a toy store at
Christmastime just for fun.

• 140 •
Discovering a shortcut to work.

• 141 •
Sticking to your New Year's resolutions.

• 142 •
Playing "cootchie coo" with a baby.

• 143 •
Reading a juicy supermarket tabloid in the
check-out line without feeling guilty.

◆ 144 ◆
Chinese fortune cookies.

◆ 145 ◆
Being told by someone you haven't seen in
years that you look younger than ever.

◆ 146 ◆
Pretending to make a coin disappear
and then magically pulling it out from behind a small child's ear.

◆ 147 ◆
Laughing so hard you cry.

◆ 148 ◆

Drinking the fresh milk from a coconut.

◆ 149 ◆

Powdering a newborn baby's bottom.

◆ 150 ◆

Watching birds frolic in a bird bath.

◆ 151 ◆

Putting money in your expired parking
meter just seconds before a policeman is
about to give you a ticket.

• 152 •
Taking a nap in a hammock.

• 153 •
Swinging as high as you can on a park
swing.

• 154 •
Dipping a piece of bread into
the spaghetti sauce.

• 155 •
Jumping into a pile of freshly raked
autumn leaves.

• 156 •
Blowing bubbles.

• 157 •
Putting your hand on the stomach
of a pregnant woman (whom you know
well) and feeling the baby kick.

• 158 •
Riding bumper cars at an amusement park.

• 159 •
Luxuriating in a sauna.

• 160 •
Watching kittens being born.

• 161 •
The first day of spring.

• 162 •
A car stopping in heavy traffic just so you
can cross the street.

• 163 •
Ice skating on a pond on a moonlit night.

• 164 •
Making funny faces at the children
who are looking out the rear window of the
car in front of you.

• 165 •
Leaving corn out for a friendly squirrel.

• 166 •
Having a secret admirer.

• 167 •
A double feature at the drive-in.

• 168 •
Carving your initials in an old oak tree.

• 169 •
Reading the Sunday funnies.

• 170 •
Keeping a photograph of your family
on your desk at work.

• 171 •
Picnicking on the living room floor when
the weather outside is nasty.

• 172 •

Turning up the heat of your electric
blanket on a cold night.

• 173 •

Tasting the salt of the ocean on your lips.

• 174 •

Not finding any police in sight
after accidentally running a red light.

• 175 •

Collecting sea shells by the seashore.

• 176 •
Taking a child to see Santa Claus.

• 177 •
Camping out in your backyard

• 178 •
Taking a hot shower first thing in the
morning.

• 179 •
Mugging for the camera with your best
friend in a photo booth.

• 180 •
Carving a jack-o'-lantern.

• 181 •
Being tickled.

• 182 •
Discovering the mailbox stuffed with
cards on your birthday.

• 183 •
Having your loved one massage your
tired, aching feet.

• 184 •
Bouncing on a trampoline.

• 185 •
Making homemade ice cream.

• 186 •
Being someone's valentine on Valentine's
Day.

• 187 •
Cracking open an egg and finding
a double yolk.

• 188 •
Flying a paper airplane that you just made.

• 189 •
Seeing a total eclipse of the sun.

• 190 •
Getting a raise without asking for one.

• 191 •
Finding out that an item you're
planning to buy has been marked down by
50 percent.

• 192 •

Eating wild berries right off the bush.

• 193 •

Watching a Slinky slink down the stairway.

• 194 •

Playing your favorite song on a jukebox.

• 195 •

Doing a "cannonball" into a pool.

• 196 •

Strolling through an art museum.

• 197 •
Sipping a glass of wine at an outdoor cafe.

• 198 •
Indian summer.

• 199 •
Whistling a happy tune.

• 200 •
Dancing an Irish jig on St. Patrick's Day.

• 201 •
Giving a piggyback ride to a small child.

• 202 •
Rubbing "Eskimo noses" with your lover.

• 203 •
Getting kinged in checkers.

• 204 •
Taking a moonlight stroll.

• 205 •
Swaying on an old-fashioned swing made
from a heavy rope and a worn tire.

• 206 •
Wearing flannel jammies on a winter night.

• 207 •
Daydreaming.

• 208 •
Going on a boat ride and singing the theme
song to "Gilligan's Island."

• 209 •
Listening to records on an old phonograph.

• 210 •
Waking up from a terrific dream and
remembering all the details.

• 211 •
Making up after a fight.

• 212 •
Someone to wash the dishes after
you've cooked the dinner.

• 213 •
Seeing the first glimpse of your baby
on the ultrasound.

LIFE'S SIMPLE PLEASURES

• 214 •
A day off from work.

• 215 •
Having enough change for a pay phone.

• 216 •
Catching a foul ball in the stands
at a baseball game.

• 217 •
Fridays at 5:00 p.m.

• 218 •
Singing a baby to sleep with a lullaby.

• 219 •
Twirling a hula hoop as long as you can.

• 220 •
The sound of a whistling tea kettle.

• 221 •
Letting out a big burp when you're full.

• 222 •
Falling asleep in your lover's arms.

• 223 •
Buying a hot pretzel
from a street vendor and eating it
all smothered with mustard.

• 224 •
Someone to scratch an itch
you can't quite reach.

• 225 •
Riding the ocean waves in an inner tube.

• 226 •
Baking your own bread from scratch.

• 227 •
Blowing out all the candles
on your birthday cake with one breath.

• 228 •
Teaching a child how to ride a bike.

• 229 •
Taking off your shoes and wading in a
public water fountain.

• 230 •
A water pistol fight.

• 231 •

Listening to the wind rustle through
the trees in a forest.

• 232 •

Seeing a movie for the bargain matinee
price.

• 233 •

Eating at an Italian restaurant that has red
checkered tablecloths adorned with candles
flickering in red jars.

• 234 •
Soft kisses.

• 235 •
Eating a ripe peach.

• 236 •
Pulling out of the driveway as you leave
on a vacation.

• 237 •
Having a good hair day.

• 238 •
Sleeping in your own bed after being
away on vacation.

• 239 •
Finding a taxi during a rainstorm.

• 240 •
Riding through a covered bridge.

• 241 •
The fragrance of a gardenia.

• 242 •
Volunteering your time at a hospital.

• 243 •
Looking at old family
photos and recalling all the good times
associated with them.

• 244 •
No lumps in your bed.

• 245 •
Bobbing for apples.

• 246 •
Making out a wish list for Christmas.

• 247 •
Dressing to the nines for a special
night on the town.

• 248 •
Hitting the bull's-eye when playing darts.

• 249 •
Learning the moves to the latest dance craze.

◆ 250 ◆

Blowing a dandelion seed and making
a wish.

◆ 251 ◆

A cup of coffee when you wake up
in the morning.

◆ 252 ◆

Buying a box of chocolate mint cookies
from a Girl Scout.

◆ 253 ◆

Hogging the covers in bed.

• 254 •
Your car heater quickly working on a
frigid day.

• 255 •
The phone remaining silent while you are
watching your favorite TV program.

• 256 •
Sleeping late on the weekend.

• 257 •
Taking a train instead of driving.

◆ 258 ◆
Doing your Christmas shopping early
to beat the rush.

◆ 259 ◆
Making a baby giggle.

◆ 260 ◆
Finding sand dollars at the bottom of the
ocean.

◆ 261 ◆
No rain the entire time you are on vacation.

• 262 •
Feeding milk to a stray kitty.

• 263 •
Being told you look like you've lost weight
after only a few days of dieting.

• 264 •
Helping somebody find a lost item.

• 265 •
Making it to the gas station with the
indicator on "Empty."

• 266 •
No line at the post office.

• 267 •
Writing your name in the sand at the beach and then watching the tide wash it away.

• 268 •
Sculpting a pot out of clay.

• 269 •
Eating cold, leftover pizza for breakfast.

• 270 •

Receiving a thank-you note.

• 271 •

Driving past a bakery and getting a whiff of
freshly baked bread.

• 272 •

Finding a really great bargain at a garage
sale.

• 273 •

Reading poetry under a big shade tree.

• 274 •

Playing "Mary Had a Little Lamb" on a
push-button phone.

• 275 •

Writing a letter, sticking it in a bottle
and tossing it into the ocean.

• 276 •

Singing Christmas carols.

• 277 •

Reading the book before seeing
the movie version.

• 278 •
Coasting on your bike down a nice
long hill.

• 279 •
Being the one to give others the good news.

• 280 •
Jumping rope with the neighborhood kids.

• 281 •
The tinkling sound of ice cubes falling
into a glass.

• 282 •
The rumbling of distant thunder
on a summer afternoon.

• 283 •
Floating on a raft in a pool.

• 284 •
Taking the back roads for a change instead
of the main streets.

• 285 •
Fresh breath.

• 286 •
Enlarging a favorite family photo
and framing it.

• 287 •
Collecting pine cones.

• 288 •
Keeping a diary of your innermost thoughts,
hopes and dreams.

• 289 •
A neighbor returning something that was
borrowed a long time ago.

• 290 •
Watching a full moon rise.

• 291 •
A supermarket checker opening up a new
register and taking you next in line.

• 292 •
Reaffirming your wedding vows in a
private ceremony for your family and close
friends.

• 293 •
Eating fresh corn on the cob.

• 294 •

Receiving a compliment from your boss
for a job well done.

• 295 •

Pressing a flower in a book.

• 296 •

Having enough time to eat a hot breakfast in
the morning before going to work.

• 297 •

Catching butterflies with a net.

• 298 •
A baby's first tooth.

• 299 •
Having candles and flashlights on
hand when the electricity suddenly goes off.

• 300 •
Getting your money's worth at a basketball
game because it went into overtime.

• 301 •
Scooping up a handful of jacks on one
bounce.

• 302 •
Watching a baby's first steps.

• 303 •
Your mother taking care of you when
you are sick.

• 304 •
Saving the cherry for last when eating
an ice cream sundae.

• 305 •
The autumn leaves turning color.

LIFE'S SIMPLE PLEASURES

• 306 •
Watching the gymnastics competition
during the Olympic Games.

• 307 •
Getting eight hours of sleep.

• 308 •
Giving the grand tour to a friend who is
visiting your town for the first time.

• 309 •
Recycling.

• 310 •
Working for a boss who asks for your
input and suggestions.

• 311 •
Caring friends.

• 312 •
The ketchup flowing out of the bottle
without your having to pound on the bottom of it.

◆ 313 ◆
Running through the lawn sprinklers
on a hot day.

◆ 314 ◆
Bringing a cooler of food and drinks
along on a long car trip and stopping mid-
way to have a picnic.

◆ 315 ◆
Watching "The Three Stooges" comedy
shorts featuring the original Curly.

• 316 •
Browsing in an old five-and-dime store.

• 317 •
Saying good morning to a
stranger and getting a cheery good morning
in return.

• 318 •
Whispering secrets in a quiet library.

• 319 •
Counting the cows on a drive through the
countryside.

• 320 •
Drinking hot apple cider.

• 321 •
Popping the "popcorn" packing material that
is stuffed into boxes to protect shipped
goods.

• 322 •
Building a tree house.

• 323 •
Chowing down on free eats at
a bar's happy hour.

• 324 •

Attending a neighborhood block party.

• 325 •

The first bite into a caramel apple.

• 326 •

Licking the bowl while making
chocolate pudding.

• 327 •

Taking your car in to a mechanic
and finding out that it can be fixed with an
inexpensive repair job.

• 328 •
Sharing an ice cream soda with two straws.

• 329 •
Burying a friend up to his neck in
the sand at the beach.

• 330 •
Drinking a beer from a cold, frosty mug.

• 331 •
Opening up a fresh can of coffee
and taking a whiff.

• 332 •
Listening to the roar of the ocean by holding
a conch shell to your ear.

• 333 •
Making shadow puppets with your hands.

• 334 •
The smell of a new car.

• 335 •
Picking out clouds that resemble
people or objects.

• 336 •
Playing volleyball on the beach with friends.

• 337 •
Listening to the raindrops
beating on your window on a stormy day.

• 338 •
Keeping a good-luck charm in your pocket.

• 339 •
Finding a penny face up, picking it up, and
all day long having good luck.

• 340 •

Driving around your neighborhood at
Christmastime to see which house has the
best display of lights.

• 341 •

Waking up to the smell of bacon
and eggs cooking.

• 342 •

Renting *Casablanca* and watching it with
someone you love.

◆ 343 ◆
Singing "Take Me Out to the Ballgame"
during the seventh-inning stretch.

◆ 344 ◆
Following a rainbow to see where it ends.

◆ 345 ◆
Bird-watching.

◆ 346 ◆
Feeling the bubbles tickle your nose when
drinking a glass of champagne.

• 347 •
Sleeping on clean sheets.

• 348 •
Warming your cold hands over a hot fire.

• 349 •
Donating your old clothes to someone less
fortunate than you are.

• 350 •
Holding the door open for the person
entering behind you.

• 351 •
Kissing your honey under the mistletoe.

• 352 •
Taking a spin in a convertible
with the top down.

• 353 •
Hot buttered popcorn at the movies.

• 354 •
Galloping on horseback.

• 355 •
Throwing rice on the wedding couple.

• 356 •
Watching Dick Clark ring in the New Year at
New York's Times Square.

• 357 •
Seeing your reflection in a pond.

• 358 •
Unwrapping a present.

• 359 •
Gaining an extra hour of sleep when you set
the clock back for standard time in the fall.

• 360 •
Being told by the dentist that your teeth
are in perfect condition.

• 361 •
The feel of silk against your skin.

• 362 •
Eating breakfast in an old-fashioned diner.

• 363 •
Having a reliable baby-sitter to watch
your kids.

• 364 •
Playing "Chopsticks" on the piano.

• 365 •
Watching the Macy's Thanksgiving Day
parade on TV while the turkey cooks in the
oven.

• 366 •
After-Christmas sales.

• 367 •
Dunking donuts in your morning coffee.

• 368 •
Being able to fit into the same size jeans
you wore in high school.

• 369 •
Having the house all to yourself.

• 370 •
Double coupons.

LIFE'S SIMPLE PLEASURES

• 371 •
Watching cartoons on Saturday morning.

• 372 •
Corresponding with a pen pal
in another country.

• 373 •
Changing your hairstyle.

• 374 •
Watching fireworks on the Fourth of July.

• 375 •

Swimming in a heated pool on a cold day.

• 376 •

Catching every green light when you're
late to work.

• 377 •

Breaking off the bigger half of the wishbone
from a turkey.

• 378 •

Doing your own thing.

• 379 •
Playing "footsie" with your main squeeze.

• 380 •
Spraying your friend with a hose while
washing the car together.

• 381 •
The good news being better than the
bad news.

• 382 •
Reading the Sunday paper in the park.

• 383 •

Reminiscing through the pages of your
high school yearbook.

• 384 •

The season's first snowfall.

• 385 •

Searching for the biggest and best pumpkin
in the pumpkin patch for Halloween.

• 386 •

Writing your name in wet cement for
posterity.

• 387 •
Waterfalls.

• 388 •
Tiptoeing through the tulips.

• 389 •
Bumming around in sloppy clothes
on the weekend.

• 390 •
Touching your toes.

• 391 •
Watching reruns of "I Love Lucy."

• 392 •
Saying grace before meals.

• 393 •
Being the designated taste tester for
the mashed potatoes.

• 394 •
Making Rice Krispies treats.

• 395 •

Getting free advice by reading a newspaper
column that discusses a problem just
like yours.

• 396 •

The smell of anything chocolate.

• 397 •

Walking in footprints that someone has
already left in the snow.

• 398 •

Clean public rest rooms.

• 399 •
Laughing at yourself.

• 400 •
Someone to greet you at the airport when
you arrive back in town.

• 401 •
Waving sparklers on the Fourth of July.

• 402 •
Licking the middle out of an Oreo cookie.

• 403 •

Buying fresh produce from a roadside stand.

• 404 •

Window shopping on a street that
has expensive stores.

• 405 •

The tinkling bells of an ice cream truck.

• 406 •

Cleaning the house in your underwear.

◆ 407 ◆
Freshly squeezed orange juice.

◆ 408 ◆
Hunting for out-of-print books in a
used-book store.

◆ 409 ◆
Remembering all the words to your
high school's alma mater.

◆ 410 ◆
Paying all your bills on time.

LIFE'S SIMPLE PLEASURES

• 411 •
A full tank of gas in your car.

• 412 •
Feeding bread to the ducks at a pond.

• 413 •
Finishing all the errands and chores
on your list.

• 414 •
Nursing a sick friend back to health.

• 415 •
Riding a bicycle built for two.

• 416 •
The smell of potpourri wafting
through the house.

• 417 •
Learning a magic trick.

• 418 •
Waking up to the sounds of birds
chirping outside.

◆ 419 ◆

Waking up thinking you have to get up,
then looking at the clock and realizing you
can sleep for a couple more hours.

◆ 420 ◆

Someone to kiss your boo-boo
and make it all better just like your mom
did when you were a kid.

◆ 421 ◆

Smooching at a drive-in movie.

• 422 •

Letting yourself have a good cry.

• 423 •

Licking your fingers after gnawing
on barbecued ribs.

• 424 •

Jack Frost nipping at your nose.

• 425 •

The prize at the bottom of a Cracker
Jack box.

• 426 •

Smelling the fragrance of the shampoo as
you lather up your hair.

• 427 •

Stuffing yourself at an all-you-can-eat buffet.

• 428 •

Flying an American flag in front of
your house.

• 429 •

Discovering a checkbook error in your favor.

• 430 •
Hearing church bells in the distance.

• 431 •
Writing a love letter to your sweetheart.

• 432 •
Keeping a journal when you
go on special trips so you can remember
what a great time you had.

• 433 •
Drinking a root beer float.

• 434 •

Seeing the skyline of your town in the
distance on a clear day.

• 435 •

Sending your mother flowers even though
it's not her birthday or Mother's Day.

• 436 •

Finding a four-leaf clover.

• 437 •

Hot chicken soup when you have a cold.

◆ 438 ◆
Enrolling in a college course just
for the fun of it.

◆ 439 ◆
Playing an April Fool's joke on a friend.

◆ 440 ◆
Windmills.

◆ 441 ◆
Taking a nap with your dog or cat
curled up at your feet.

• 442 •
Talcum powder in your shoes.

• 443 •
Serenading your lover.

• 444 •
Growing a vegetable garden.

• 445 •
Planting a tree in memory of a loved one
who has passed away.

• 446 •

Serving Thanksgiving dinner at a shelter
for the homeless.

• 447 •

Catching fireflies in a jar.

• 448 •

Taking home videos.

• 449 •

Rolling three strikes in a row—a turkey—
when bowling.

• 450 •
Looking up your favorite teacher
from high school.

• 451 •
Singing in the church choir.

• 452 •
Making s'mores on a camping trip.

• 453 •
The sun shining through stained-glass
windows.

• 454 •

Picking out your next pet from the pound.

• 455 •

Doing something nice for someone without
expecting anything in return.

• 456 •

Singing in the shower.

• 457 •

Finding your way in a strange city just when
it seems you are hopelessly lost.

• 458 •
Peering through a kaleidoscope.

• 459 •
Someone taking your advice—and
having it work out.

• 460 •
A child's artwork taped to the refrigerator.

• 461 •
Buying a fancy dinner with the loose change
you've been saving in your piggy bank.

• 462 •
Watching the sun come back out
after a nasty rainstorm.

• 463 •
Dancing cheek to cheek.

• 464 •
Going to a high school or college football
game and rooting for your alma mater.

• 465 •
Rereading your favorite book.

◆ 466 ◆
The smell of a cedar chest.

◆ 467 ◆
Watching the faces of small children
as they open their presents on Christmas
morning.

◆ 468 ◆
Attending your high school reunion.

◆ 469 ◆
Nonsmoking restaurants.

◆ 470 ◆
Stopping to help someone whose car
has broken down by the side of the road.

◆ 471 ◆
Reading the Bible.

◆ 472 ◆
Waking up to a rooster's "cock-a-doodle-
doo."

◆ 473 ◆
Having a best friend.

• 474 •

Watching an inchworm cross the sidewalk.

• 475 •

Reciting "The Pledge of Allegiance."

• 476 •

Someone else volunteering to walk the dog
when it's raining outside.

• 477 •

A good-night kiss.

• 478 •
Buying gifts for family and friends at a
local arts-and-crafts show instead of at the
mall.

• 479 •
Trimming the Christmas tree.

• 480 •
Hearing from an old friend you haven't
seen in years.

• 481 •
Doing a cartwheel.

◆ 482 ◆

Eating an ordinary dinner on your
good china.

◆ 483 ◆

Falling asleep to your favorite music
on the radio.

◆ 484 ◆

A bonfire at the beach.

◆ 485 ◆

Making a sale on the first call in response to
your classified ad in the newspaper.

• 486 •

The sun beating down on your face.

• 487 •

Coaxing a parrot into saying your name.

• 488 •

Listening to your parents tell stories about
when they were young.

• 489 •

Going door to door in the neighborhood to
collect money for a worthy charity.

• 490 •
Being in a good mood.

• 491 •
Playing "20 Questions" and "GHOST" to
help pass the time on a car trip.

• 492 •
Playing fetch with a dog.

• 493 •
Learning a new word every day to add
to your vocabulary.

LIFE'S SIMPLE PLEASURES

◆ 494 ◆

Being able to breathe again after a cold.

◆ 495 ◆

Watching a funny TV show when you
are feeling blue.

◆ 496 ◆

Getting a free sample at the bakery.

◆ 497 ◆

A short wait at the doctor's office.

◆ 498 ◆
Sinking down into an overstuffed sofa.

◆ 499 ◆
Receiving a postcard from a friend who is
on vacation.

◆ 500 ◆
Fitting the final piece into a jigsaw puzzle.

◆ 501 ◆
Stopping to smell the roses.

WHAT ARE SOME OF YOUR SIMPLEST PLEASURES?

Do you have a simple pleasure that you would like to share with our readers? If so, we may use it in a future edition of our book and give you credit for suggesting it! Send your life's simple pleasures to the following address:

LIFE'S SIMPLE PLEASURES
1227 West Magnolia, Suite 500
Fort Worth, Texas 76104

All material becomes the property of the authors of this book and is non-returnable. Thank you for participating!